I've Got a Secret!   I've Got a Secret!   I've Got a Secret!   I've Got a Secret!

I've Got a Secret!   I've Got a Secret!   I've Got a Secret!   I've Got a Secret!

I've Got a Secret!   I've Got a Secret!   I've Got a Secret!   I've Got a Secret!

This book belongs to:

_____

_____

I've Got a Secret!   I've Got a Secret!   I've Got a Secret!   I've Got a Secret!

I've Got a Secret!   I've Got a Secret!   I've Got a Secret!   I've Got a Secret!

This book is not just ABOUT secrets, the pages have a secret of their own for you to find. Follow the code at the end of the book to find out the secret.

Copyright © Wendy Francis 2020
ALL RIGHTS RESERVED

Published in 2020 by Connor Court Publishing Pty Ltd
Connor Court Publishing Pty Ltd
PO Box 7257
Redland Bay QLD 4165

sales@connorcourt.com
www.connorcourtpublishing.com.au

ISBN: 9781922449399

Front Cover Design: Tim Weatherall
Front Cover Picture: Joy Weatherall
Picture Credits: Joy Weatherall
Printed in Australia

I've Got a Secret!

Written by Wendy Francis

Illustrated by Joy Weatherall

Connor Court Publishing

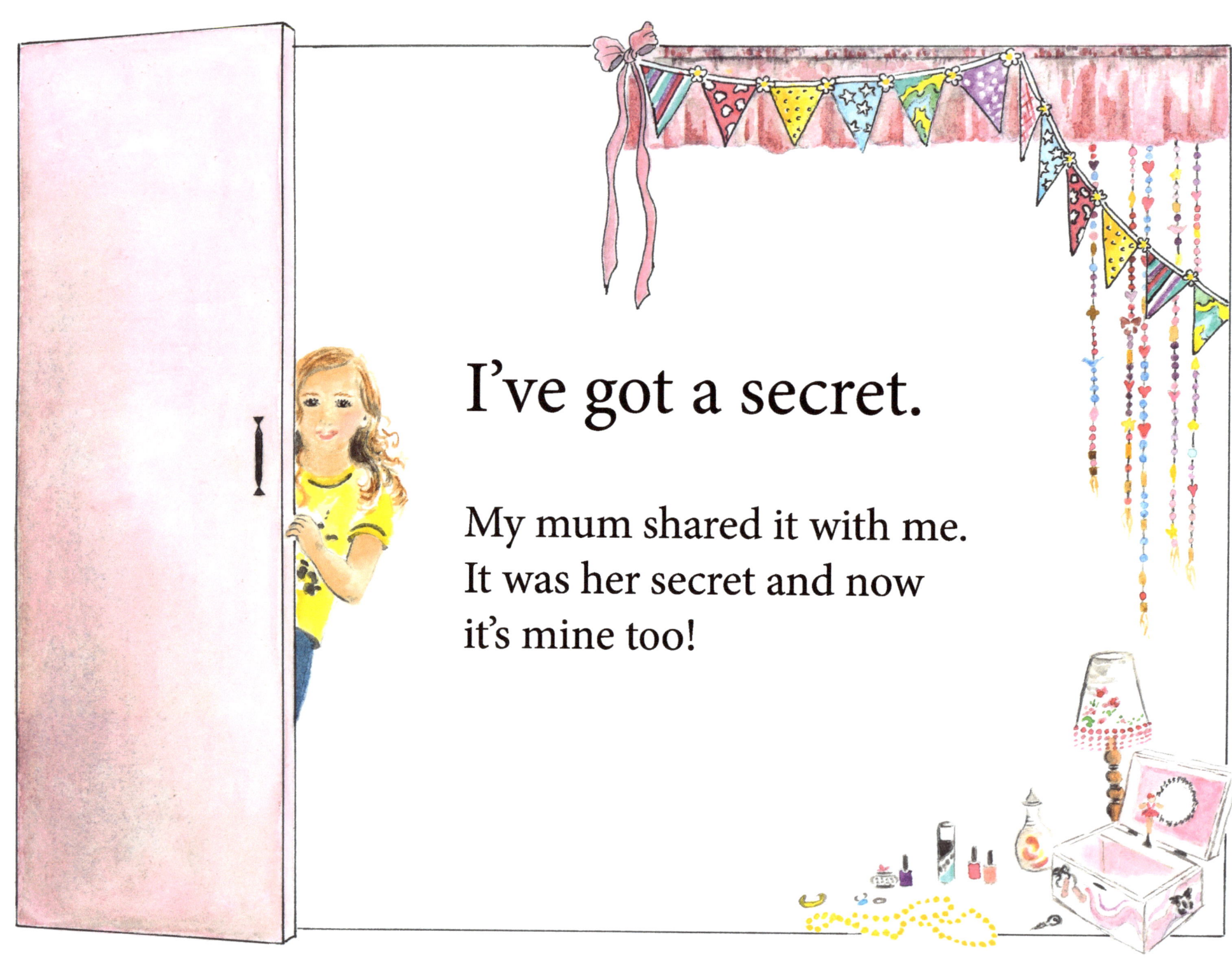

I've got a secret.

My mum shared it with me.
It was her secret and now
it's mine too!

Can you guess what it is?

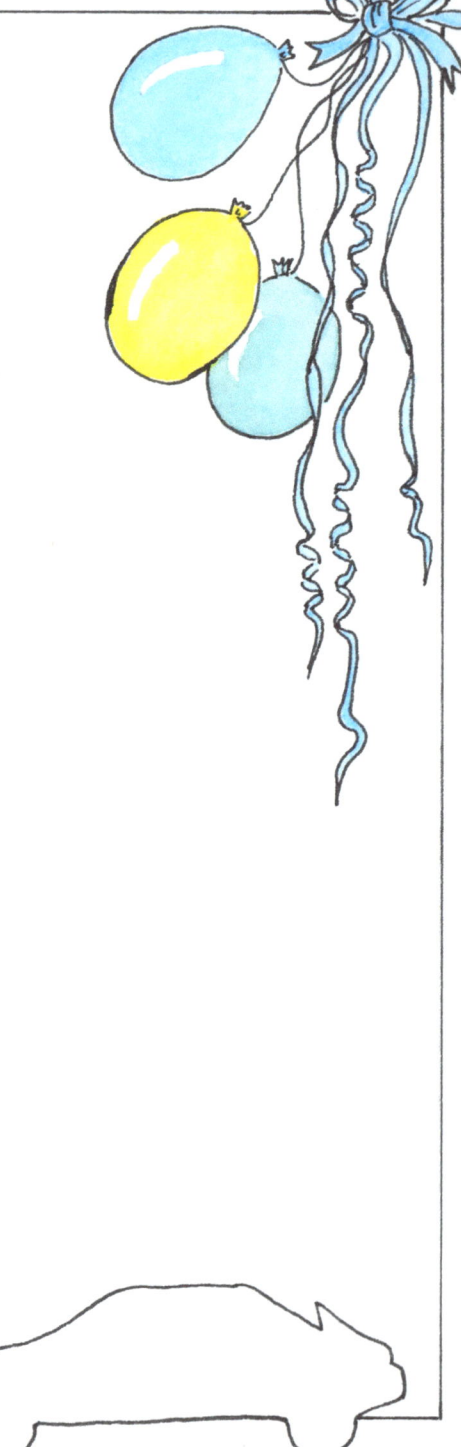

It's a birthday present for my brother.

I helped Mum hide it in my bedroom cupboard so that he wouldn't know about it until his special day.
He'll be very happy when he finds out.
It makes me want to tell him now!

But it's a secret, so I will wait until his special day. He's going to be very surprised. It will be a lot of fun. Having a secret like this

is exciting!

SURPRISE

After mum and I hid my brother's present she talked to me about secrets. She told me that there are good secrets, like birthday and Christmas presents, surprise parties, treasure hunts, baby and wedding announcements. Sometimes there is family news that we keep secret until we let others know. But she said that I needed to know that some things should never be kept secret.

Mum said that if something makes you afraid, or sad, or uncomfortable, it shouldn't be kept a secret. She also said that it was never right for someone to ask me to keep something a secret to keep them out of trouble. She taught me some rhyming words to remember.

What she said made a lot of sense to me.

I was so glad mum explained secrets to me because it helped me understand something that happened the next week at school.

One of my friends seemed sad.

In the morning when she came to school,
it looked like she had been crying.

At lunch break, she didn't feel like joining in our usual games. Then, when I asked her what was wrong, she said she couldn't tell me, because it was a secret.

I knew just what to do! I told her what my mum had said to me about secrets. It made sense to her too! I offered to go with her to speak to our teacher straight away. I was sure our teacher would be able to help. My friend promised instead that she would tell her parents the secret after school.

HOME →

When a secret makes you sad,
If it makes you worried or mad,
It's not good, it's very bad!
So tell an adult, or Mum or Dad.

That night my friend's mother called my mum on the phone to thank her for the rhyme I had shared at school that day.

It felt so good to have been able to help my friend.

When a secret makes you sad,
If it makes you worried or mad,
It's not good, it's very bad!
So tell an adult, or Mum or Dad.

The next day at school my friend was so happy.

She didn't tell me everything about what had happened, but she said that the secret had been about someone who had been visiting her home. They had done something awful to her and then made her promise not to tell anyone!

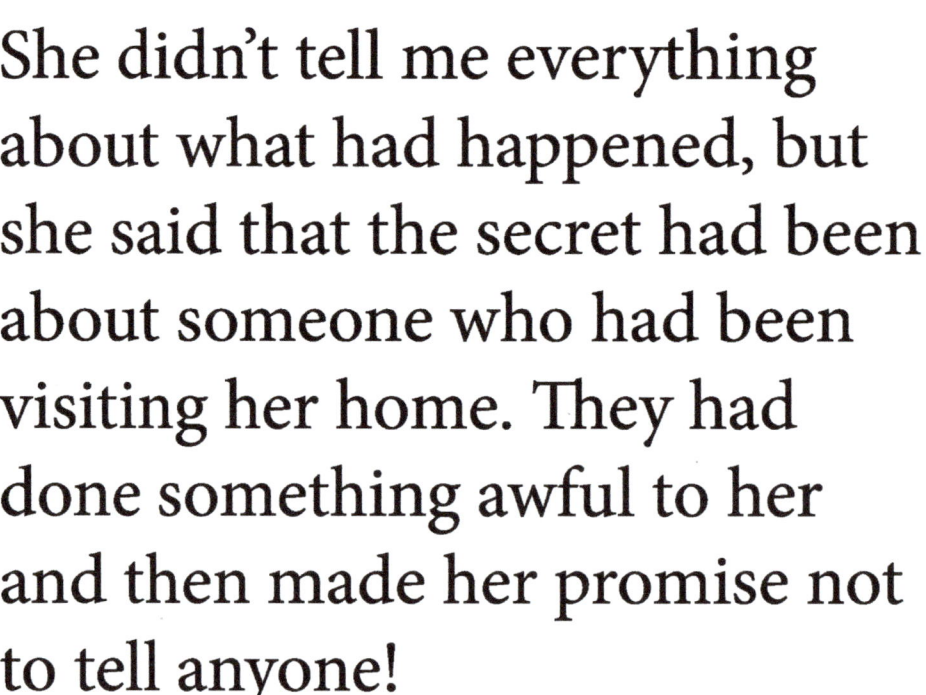

My friend was so glad she told her parents everything. She knows that they love her and now that they know, they will be able to protect her.

Telling them the secret was the right thing to do.

I'm sure that at Christmas and birthday times, and other special occasions, my family will still have lots of fun secrets. But not the sort that hurt. **Good secrets bring happy surprises when they are told.**

Do you want to know a secret?

It's hidden in the pages of this book!
You can find it by following this code.

Follow this code to find a special six word secret hidden in the book.

Page 24	1st Word	1st Letter	___
Page 4	7th Word	2nd Letter	___
Page 10	4th Word	5th Letter	___
Page 12	10th Word	1st Letter	___
Page 14	8th Word	3rd Letter	___
Page 8	10th Word	2nd Letter	___
Page 10	1st Word	3rd Letter	___
Page 16	12th Word	1st Letter	___
Page 15	1st Word	1st Letter	___
Page 20	5th Word	2nd Letter	___
Page 20	11th Word	5th Letter	___
Page 22	8th Word	3rd Letter	___
Page 23	3rd Word	1st Letter	___
Page 12	7th Word	6th Letter	___
Page 24	2nd Word	5th Letter	___
Page 23	5th Word	1st Letter	___
Page 16	3rd Word	2nd Letter	___
Page 10	9th Word	1st Letter	___
Page 26	7th Word	1st Letter	___
Page 28	8th Word	3rd Letter	___
Page 30	10th Word	4th Letter	___
Page 20	6th Word	2nd Letter	___

_ _ _ _   _ _ _ _ _ _ _   _ _ _ _ _   _ _ _ _   _ _ _ _ _ _   _ _ _ _ _

Note to parents

One of a parent's most important responsibilities is to teach their child the difference between what is good and what is bad. That can be made more difficult, and can be confusing for children, when something can be both good AND bad depending on the circumstances. This is the case with secrets. We've all known the joy of having a secret that we are holding onto until the right time to reveal it – birthday and Christmas presents, a special date, a surprise holiday or party. These are exciting secrets that make life fun and interesting.

Sadly, not all secrets are fun, or bring joy. They can be destructive and life altering. Silence is a tool used by abusers to bully children into keeping the abuse 'their little secret', encouraging them not to tell anyone about it, or even threatening that they will get in trouble if they tell. Far too often, these cruel tactics work.

It's vitally important that we teach our children the difference between a good secret that leads to a happy surprise, and a bad secret that covers up wrong. Secrets that make a child feel uncomfortable, or worried, or sad – these should never be kept to themselves.

As you read this book with your child, my hope is that it will help you to start a bigger conversation. We want them to feel safe to tell us absolutely anything.

- Encourage your child never to keep a secret from you unless it is a fun surprise that is going to be revealed at the right time.
- Tell your child that you want to know about anything that hurts them, or makes them feel uncomfortable. If someone touches them, or looks at their private parts, that must never be a secret. They need to know that they should immediately tell you or a trusted adult.
- If a friend tells them a secret, they should also tell you or a trusted adult, so that you can take the appropriate action.
- Make sure your child knows that it is never their fault if someone does something bad to them, and that they will not be in trouble for telling you. You need to know. You want to know because you love them and will protect them.

Sometimes we assume that our children understand things when they really don't! Secrets can be confusing for children. Knowing the difference between a good secret and a bad secret can save them from life-affecting trauma. I encourage you to not only read this book to them, but to keep the conversation going. Open and ongoing communication with our children is key.

Wendy Francis

I've Got a Secret!   I've Got a Secret!   I've Got a Secret!   I've Got a Secret!

I've Got a Secret!   I've Got a Secret!   I've Got a Secret!   I've Got a Secret!

I've Got a Secret!   I've Got a Secret!   I've Got a Secret!   I've Got a Secret!

I've Got a Secret!   I've Got a Secret!   I've Got a Secret!   I've Got a Secret!

I've Got a Secret!   I've Got a Secret!   I've Got a Secret!   I've Got a Secret!

I've Got a Secret!   I've Got a Secret!   I've Got a Secret!   I've Got a Secret!

www.ingramcontent.com/pod-product-compliance
Lightning Source LLC
Chambersburg PA
CBHW041951150426

43195CB00004B/106